The Scanning Patterns of Human Infants: Implications for Visual Learning

MONOGRAPHS ON INFANCY

Lewis P. Lipsitt, Editor

**TODDLERS' BEHAVIORS WITH AGEMATES:
ISSUES OF INTERACTION, COGNITION,
AND AFFECT**
Wanda C. Bronson

**THE SCANNING PATTERNS OF HUMAN INFANTS:
IMPLICATIONS FOR VISUAL LEARNING**
Gordon W. Bronson

The Scanning Patterns of Human Infants: Implications for Visual Learning

Gordon W. Bronson
Mills College
Oakland, California

with a commentary by
Richard N. Aslin

ABLEX PUBLISHING CORPORATION
Norwood, NJ 07648

Printed in the United States of America.

Library of Congress Cataloging in Publication Data

Bronson, Gordon, W.
  The scanning patterns of human infants.

  (Monographs on infancy)
  Includes bibliographical references and index.
  1. Visual perception in children.   2. Infant
psychology.   I. Title.   II. Series.
BF720.V57B76   155.4′2   81-20543
ISBN 0-89391-114-3   AACR2

ABLEX Publishing Corporation
355 Chestnut Street
Norwood, New Jersey 07648

Contents

Acknowledgments

Completion of this study was made possible only through the contributions of a number of individuals. Mark Bronson provided intelligent enthusiasm for the original notion of building an eye-tracking device, and subsequently developed the software for the system; Alex Para designed and Steve Lones installed the necessary electronics. John Watson and Ervin Hafter generously lent the computer facilities within their respective laboratories, for system development and for the use of a computer within the fully developed system. Georgia Chourré helped in organizing the data collection, and in later coding of the computer-processed records. Discussions with James Bergen did much to shape the thinking about the data; Richard Aslin and my wife, Wanda Bronson, contributed detailed critiques of initial manuscripts. Finally, I am indebted to the parents who allowed me to study their infants, and who cheerfully donated their time in helping to create the data base for the project. A grant from the National Institute of Child Health and Human Development, which supported this work (HD 12565), also is gratefully acknowledged.

Preface

This is the second of a series of hard-covered volumes published as *Monographs on Infancy*. The first was that of Wanda C. Bronson, entitled "Toddlers' Behaviors with Agemates: Issues of Interaction, Cognition, and Affect."

It is a pleasure to introduce this volume by another Bronson. Gordon Bronson, a dedicated behavioral scientist, has devoted over 20 years to understanding the development of the human nervous system. The present manuscript is a significant achievement in his career, as indicated by both the Foreword author, Philip Salapatek, and the author of an extended Commentary at the conclusion of the volume, Richard Aslin. It is a matter of pride for me as Editor of *Monographs on Infancy* that Professor Bronson has elected to publish his work here.

The *Monographs* constitute one component of a tripartite publishing program on infancy begun in 1978 by Ablex Publishing Corporation under my editorial direction. Another part is the journal, *Infant Behavior and Development*, in its fifth volume as this monograph appears. The third part is the *Advances in Infancy Research* series, the first annual volume of which appeared in 1981.

The relatively brief research articles appearing in the journal are nicely complemented, we hope, by the two other styles of publication. The *Advances* are intended for intermediate size manuscripts which are critical syntheses of specialized research areas, usually capitalizing upon, but not limited, to the results of the authors' own programmatic research. The *Advances* are intended as collations of data and inferences, not principally as repositories of primary data which are best submitted to journals. The *Monographs*, on the other hand, are for longer manuscripts and usually will report original data. They are also for reports of extended research programs and collaborations. All three publication styles involve editorial scrutiny, including judgments of research experts other than the Editor. In the *Monographs* series, comments by other experts in the area circumscribed by the Monographs are solicited to provide the basis of a Foreward or of a concluding Commentary or, as in this volume, both.

We welcome and will review seriously good innovative ideas that report or promote progress in the scientific study of infant behavior and development. We will not be bound by any traditions that do not yet exist. Our policy is to attract and publish high quality manuscripts which will be reviewed and commented upon by established experts on infancy.

From the start it has been our intent to fill publication needs of developmental investigators in the fields both of human and animal infancy. The animal ethologist and developmental psychologist, Frans X. Plooij of The Netherlands, has written a beautiful manuscript, based on his extensive data, on "The Behavioral Development of Free-Living Chimpanzee Babies and Infants." Masterfully illustrated by David Bygott, this will appear in 1982 as the third entry in this *Monographs on Infancy* series.

It has been our pleasure to work with Gordon Bronson in the development of this volume, and we both hope that its appearance will serve as a stimulant for further thought and research on the early development of visual mechanisms and neural processes.

Lewis P. Lipsitt, Editor

Department of Psychology, and
Child Study Center
Brown University
Providence, R. I. 02912

Foreword

Philip Salapatek
University of Minnesota

This unpretentious monograph represents in a most explicit way the excellent developmental application of a methodology used to determine the thoughts of man since antiquity. The methodology is rooted in the assumption that the human looks in the direction of greatest visual interest. For the newborn with little memory, the physical properties of the external stimulus pretty much account for the direction of looking. For the older and increasingly mindful infant, looking is directed toward meaningful stimuli with more arbitrary physical features. Finally, at some point in infancy looking can index either voluntary attention or even active avoidance of visual events. Gordon Bronson provides an intriguing glimpse at the stages of infant visual attention.

Modern experimental interest in the developmental relationship between looking and perceiving perhaps began at the close of the 19th century, when acute observers such as C. Darwin, F. H. Champneys, G. S. Hall, M. G. Blanton, A. Genzmer, M. W. Shinn, and W. Preyer, among many others, noted infant visual preferences for brightness, color and pattern. R. L. Fantz correctly receives credit for refining their measure of gauging visual preference on the basis of direction of eye orientation, by looking more exactly at the location of the corneal reflex in the eye with respect to the pupillary reflex. He did this as a systematic function of theoretically meaningful and systematic pattern variations in the stimulus. It was the choice of the right stimuli at a theoretically opportune time that allowed him to usher in a new era of infant perception.

I think that the major methodological advance in visual investigation, the advance that provided the impetus for an examination of

visual scanning as opposed to visual preference, came simultane-
ously from Maurice Hershenson working with human infants and
Alan Cowey with monkeys during the very early 1960's. They dem-
onstrated that it was possible to successively photograph the eye
while it changed fixation, and to then determine the line of sight
from each photograph on the basis of the deviation of the corneal
from the pupillary reflex. Of course, eye fixations had been photo-
graphically determined before by many researchers, but their research was with older subjects and used optical techniques that de-
manded bite-board head restraint. Hershenson and Cowey's major
methodological contribution lay in measuring the corneal reflex in
relation to the pupillary reflex. For a given fixation point this relationship did not change through a considerable ($\pm$ 1.5 cm) head ex-
cursion, if the observer's eye or camera lay on the same image plane
as the stimulus. Thus, Hershenson and Cowey made it possible to
determine the line of sight in an infant with only mild head restraint. The successive eye fixations, moreover, remained on a per-
manent film record.

Hershenson was a student of William Kessen. So were
Marshall Haith and I. We refined the foregoing techniques in the
1960's to allow rapid successive sampling of eye positions with reasonably rapid measurement of the corneal and pupillary reflexes.
Many automated corneal photographic devices existing today, that
allow head movement and are suitable for infants, are some refine-
ment of the foregoing model. This model has allowed the collection
of data on visual scanning, including a reasonable sample of fairly
accurate successive fixations, as opposed to assessment of simple
visual preference as in a right-left or yes-no fixation paradigm.

Surprisingly, very few investigators have systematically collected visual scanning data from infants since the technology was
developed. Obvious obstacles to doing so include the expense of the
equipment, the difficulty of the photography, and most especially
the tedium of data reduction and analysis. Less obvious but even
more important difficulties, I think, are theoretical. The visual
scanning technique in the 1960's was a new toy. Every encounter
with it produced a delightful insight. From the vantage point of the
infant's retina we marvelled at the piecemeal, and sometimes extensive, manner in which the very young infant scanned every pattern placed before her. There were regularities: a looser scan on a
given feature at a younger age, a broader horizontal scan, an early
concern with external and a later concern with internal features.

more extensive scanning with age. The details of these generalizations continue to be worked out, but they all tend to have two things in common. They are descriptive, and are based on spontaneous preferences. Thus, they have tapped processes involving detection and discrimination, but only if there are preferred elements. For this reason larger questions regarding perceptual learning and memory resulting from scanning have remained largely untouched within these paradigms; for example, does looking result in memory and memory in decrements in looking? On the other hand, some ingenious non-scanning habituation studies, e.g., by Allen Milewski and by I. W. R. Bushnell, have looked at discriminations involving memory based on hypotheses derived from the visual scanning data of others.

Thus, we have had a paradoxical state of affairs. The visual scanning studies have often produced systematic patterns of visual investigation that seem certainly to be related to memory. On the other hand, many habituation studies have produced powerful demonstrations of memory that seem certain to be based on visual investigation. However, no one has consistently put together the mechanism and construct in visual scanning studies during the 1970's. This union is the next logical step in making visual scanning (and not simply visual choice) studies worthwhile.

Gordon Bronson appears to be on the right track in this small, but elegant study. What he has attempted goes well beyond the basic task of explaining stimulus detection, discrimination and memory as a function of the physical stimulus present. Rather, he seeks to answer *how* detection, discrimination, and memory are accomplished, as well as what is accomplished. This goal leads him to translate variations in duration of fixation, length of saccades, individual scanning patterns, and changes in scanning over repeated presentations, into psychological processing components such as detection, attention, encoding of relative location, assimilation of current content, preprogramming of forthcoming saccades, visual arousal and alertness, recursive scanning or scanpaths, sequential processing, disattending or avoiding attending, and habituation. Certainly this interplay between mechanism and construct would find favor in anyone's theory of visual processing.

Bronson is not content to stop with this elaborate explication of the schema underlying infant visual perception. As has been his custom in the past, he shifts freely to a different level of analysis to examine the substrate (material) of which the psychological mecha-

nisms are built. Thus, we are offered his best guesses as to the neurophysiology underlying the psychology observed, and the psychology that should follow from the known neurophysiology. Central
and peripheral visual processing are related to the development of
central and peripheral retina, midbrain and cortex. So also are
saccadic eye movements developmentally related to cortical and
subcortical centers. X- and Y- cells are related both to eye movement control and to attention and habituation.

There are not very many developmentalists who have dared to
comprehensively examine the genesis of visual perception at both
the pyschological and neurophysiological levels, with an emphasis
on detailing the mechanisms at both levels. Certainly very few have
done a very good job at it. But this is a noble enterprise! In knowing
each psychological step, as well as its physical underpinning, we are
in a better heuristic position to learn more about both levels, and to
fix or alter the system in two ways (physical and psychological)
rather than in only a single way.

Bronson's approach to visual perception is very much like that
of Donald Hebb. There is a wise concern for exact, basic psychology; the same for neurophysiology; and there is an attempt to formulate the working relationship between the two. Of course both
attempts will become dated, but they force us for some time to consider explicitly the way things might be, and leave us with some
models of the way things are.

The Scanning Patterns of Human Infants: Implications for Visual Learning

1

Introduction

Visual information comes in a series of temporally discrete packages, each image lasting on the order of one-half second. For the knowledgeable adult, each separate image will activate memories of similar previous events; in consequence, the information gleaned from the single fixation can offer provisional clues as to the nature of the whole. In effect, for an adult a vast store of visual memories provides structure for the synthesis of successive visual images. For the ignorant infant, however, the store of visual memories will be limited, and, initially, absent—and hence the task of perceptual synthesis must proceed largely on the basis of information that has been gathered during the current experience. It follows that for the very young infant—much more than for the adult—the quality of a visual impression must depend to a large degree on the manner in which the stimulus has been scanned. It might be expected, for example, that the nature of an infant's impression will depend upon the selection of stimulus features that have been sampled, and on the patternings of re-fixations directed to particular stimulus components. At present there is almost no empirically based information which bears upon issues of this sort. It is a premise of the present study that the close examination of infant scanning patterns should begin to fill this gap, and hence shed light on the processes, and the products, of early visual learning.

Two kinds of information are required if one is to draw inferences about an infant's visual impressions from data regarding scanning patterns. First, one must know something about just how encoding processes might be linked to scanning parameters—for example, about the size of the visual area that might be assimilated during each fixation, and about the number of re-fixations required for effective encoding. Second, one also must know just how infants actually scan the visual field: whether they tend to concentrate attention on a single feature, or to scan broadly; and how scanning patterns might depend upon the physical characteristics of the stimulus, or change with continued examination. As an approach to these numerous issues, the present study has examined in considerable detail the several major parameters of infant scanning under a number of different stimulus conditions. From the way in which these parameters varied as a function of the age of the infant and of the characteristics of the stimulus, it has indeed proved possible to draw some provisional inferences regarding both the process of encoding and the nature of the recorded impressions. Readers will find, however, that not all inferences are of equal status. Some appear fairly certain, while others are, at present, but plausible hypotheses.

On the assumption that visual learning begins to be reasonably effective by around 2 months of age, this exploratory study has focused on the 2- to 5-month period. Although the sample of ten infants is relatively small, the recording of nearly every visual fixation during about 1 1/2 minutes of experimental exposure has produced a rather extensive data base—and, fortunately, most of the reported regularities proved to be sufficiently strong to support generalizations to the larger population. Two qualifications must be added, however. First, statements regarding the age of onset of new scanning characteristics necessarily are based on the data from only a few infants, and therefore the ages specified must be regarded as approximate. On the other hand, the proposed developmental sequences can be considered relatively firm. Second, it will be shown that the scanning patterns of infants are closely linked to stimulus characteristics. One must be cautious, therefore, in generalizing from present findings to other visual circumstances. Uncertainties in this latter regard are discussed at several points in the text.

Because the study produced a rather large number of significant results it seemed best to interpose discussions as each new finding is presented. Therefore, within the Results section the various parameters of scanning are presented and then discussed in a series of separate subsections. A tentative synthesis of the various findings is offered in the Discussion. Here the present findings are supplemented by previously published data collected on younger infants in order to formulate a developmental model which outlines the growth of scanning capabilities from birth up to around 5 months of age. On the basis of this provisional model, inferences then are drawn regarding the probable nature of visual learning by infants of various ages. The Appendix discusses technical issues associated with the application of an eye-tracking system to infant subjects. Information regarding the precision of measurement and the reliability of the data can be found in this part of the monograph.

2

Method

PROCEDURE

A major difficulty in applying eye-tracking techniques to infant subjects lies in keeping the pupil of the eye within the camera field, since off-camera intervals must be minimized if the scanning record is to be reasonably complete. Therefore a technique was developed which maintained the recorded eye in a near constant location as the infant rotated his head in order to scan the visual field. The infant lay in a padded crib with the head fitted snugly in a separate cradle device. The cradle was pivoted to allow the baby to rotate his or her head (plus cradle) freely from side to side, but, since the axis of cradle rotation was set to pass through the videorecorded eye, as the head turned the eye remained in a relatively fixed position. The arrangement worked well, except when the infant decided to look entirely away from the frontal area—and the likelihood of that was minimized by the design of the stimulus (see below).

Following a brief discussion of the aims and procedures of the experiment, the mother placed her infant in the crib/cradle device and interacted until the infant was content. Then the room lights were dimmed, the cradle and infant were slid into view of the camera, and the mother moved to the side of the apparatus where she again was visible to her infant. Camera adjustments were quickly made, the videorecorder was started, and the experiment now began, with the baby viewing mother's face oriented upright at a distance of about 50 cm (the mother's face was located in a predetermined position by means of a chin rest). After some 10 seconds of recording the infant's scanning of mother's face, the lights illuminating her face were turned off and the projector carrying the first experimental stimulus was turned on. From the infant's perspective, this resulted in mother's face immediately being replaced by the experimental stimulus; infants showed only continued interest during this perhaps unusual shift in visual images. (The arrangement which allowed for these rapid stimulus changes is illustrated in Figure 1 of the Appendix.)

The illuminated experimental figures appeared on a rear projection screen located 34 cm above the infant. To the dark-adapted adult, the outer boundary of the 30 cm × 30 cm screen was just detectable; apart from this, the only contours visible to the infant during the following experimental sequence were those of the projected images, together with the dim red disk of the infrared (IR) light source (the latter is a necessary part of the eye-tracking unit).

EXPERIMENTAL STIMULI

The two slightly different stimulus sets, which were seen by different groups of infants, are shown in Figure 1. A number of methodological considerations dictated the general characteristics of the stimulus sets. In each format, the dull red disk of the IR light source, together with the dimly illuminated 5 × 5 checkerboard, were present continuously, whereas the remaining more brightly illuminated figures periodically disappeared and reappeared over the series of experimental episodes (see below). The intent in having the two dim figures continuously present in the visual periphery was to offer alternative targets for fixation, should an infant be inclined to look away from the major experimental stimuli. Without such peripheral elements, it was found that an infant who was seeking additional stimuli often would turn completely away from the display area, with the result that the infant's eye would move off camera. The experimental sequence was the same for each stimulus format: first the small moving target was visible, as it traversed back and forth horizontally for one 4-second cycle (see Figure 1); then, coincident with its disappearance, the set of square experimental figures appeared for a 5-second viewing interval. This

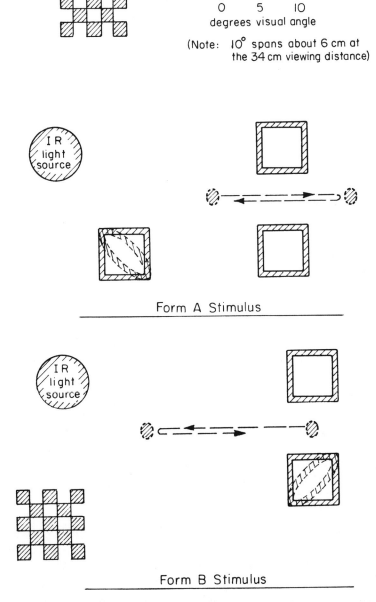

Scale

0   5   10
degrees visual angle

(Note: 10° spans about 6 cm at
the 34 cm viewing distance)

Form A Stimulus

Form B Stimulus

Figure 1. Experimental stimuli, Forms A and B. In each format, the IR light source and the checkerboard element were continuously visible; other elements reappeared periodically. The path of the small moving target is indicated by the dashed lines; the dotted elliptical shapes replaced the square figures in some episodes. See text for details.

7

sequence—moving target, then a set of static figures—continued to repeat a number of times, thus providing a series of 5-second experimental episodes separated by intervening presentations of the moving target. Three considerations dictated this experimental paradigm. First, the interspersed periods of motion effectively maintained infants' attention over the series of experimental episodes. Second, since almost without exception the infants attempted to follow the moving target, this effectively placed their fixations in a near-constant location just prior to each re-presentation of the static experimental figures. Third, the multiple sets of tracking data, collected as the infants followed the moving target, provided an extensive base for calibrating the eye-tracking unit (this rather complex procedure is discussed in the Appendix).

Several further methodological considerations contributed to decisions regarding the particular qualities of the stimulus sets. To maximize detection, the widths of figure contours were set at 1 degree, which is near the peak of the contrast sensitivity curve for infants of the present ages (see Banks & Salapatek, 1981). Stimulus intensities were kept relatively low, to avoid possible aversive reactions to the sudden appearances of the figures. (In foot-lamberts: moving target, 1.3; squares, and ellipses, .03; checkerboard, .01; background, essentially zero. These values should place the figures toward the lower end of the range of photopic sensitivity. The effective luminance of the dimly visible IR source could not be determined, since the spectral sensitivity curve for infants is unknown; to an adult it appeared slightly less bright than the square figures.) The spacings and the sizes of the various figures were dictated by the precision of the eye-tracking system. Given an ability to specify the locus of fixation to within about 3 degrees of visual angle, the present spacings allowed for the unambiguous determination of which (if any) figure was being looked at during each fixation. And with an ability to detect *changes* in the locus of fixation of between 1 and 2 degrees, with figures of these sizes it was possible to determine when a series of fixations were being directed to several different locations within the same feature.

Beyond the above methodological considerations, the forms of the stimulus sets were dictated by the theoretical aims of the study. A number of discrete elements were required, in order to detect possible age-related changes in propensities to scan over a variety of features. On the other hand, to see if there might be meaningful changes in scanning parameters following repeated exposures, it was desirable that the arrays be relatively noncomplex and hence likely soon to become "familiar." The sets of several dispersed square figures seemed to meet these requirements. In addition, it was of interest to see whether, or how soon, infants of different ages would show signs of detecting a change in the shape of one feature within the visual field. Therefore, within each stimulus format one of the square figures periodically was replaced by an elliptical shape for one of the 5-second presentations, and then returned to a square in the episode which followed (see Figure 1); the sequence of changes occurred three times within the series of episodes. Notice that the periodic change was located somewhat peripherally in the Form A stimulus, whereas in Form B it occurred in a location closely adjacent to the infants' locus of fixation at the moment of presentation. The detection of change, therefore, should have been an easier task in the Form B format.[1] The length of the experimental sequence differed slightly between the two series. If S represents episodes in which the elements remained as squares, and E those in which an ellipse was introduced, the Form A sequence was SSESSSESSSE, while for Form B it was SSESSESSE. The intent was simply to shorten the experimental procedure when the latter series was devised; as will be shown below, for the issues under analysis this difference could not have biased the relevant findings.

To summarize briefly. In each stimulus format the infants viewed a repeating set of illuminated square figures, with each 5-second presentation being separated by the traverse of the small moving target; and, three times during the series of episodes, one of the square figures was replaced by an elliptical form. The relatively dim checkerboard, together with the dim IR light source, remained continuously visible in the periphery of the stimulus field.

[1]As was anticipated, infants generally devoted more attention to the upper half of the visual field, so introducing the ellipse into a lower location enhanced the probability of demonstrating the nonchance nature of fixations directed to the changed element. It proved unnecessary to run a control series in which squares and ellipses were reversed; the infants did indeed look more at the elliptical form, but the nature of the results will infirm the notion that this might be attributed only to a "preference" for elliptical shapes.

SUBJECTS

The ten subjects ranged from 2 to 5 months of age. The ages were similar for the six infants who viewed stimulus Form A and for the four who were shown Form B. (Form A mean 3 3/4 months, range 2 to 4 3/4 months; Form B mean 3 1/2 months, range 2 1/2 to 5 months.) Since only two of the subjects were female (one in each experimental group), there will be no analysis by sex. All appeared to be normal healthy infants, and they came from essentially middle-class backgrounds. The three additional infants who were eliminated from the study should not have selectively biased the remaining sample: one 2-month-old went to sleep; the record of a 4-month-old contained, for technical reasons, large sections of missing data; and a 5-month-old began to cry shortly after the experimental sequence was introduced (the reason for this is of interest, and this additional infant is included in one section of the results which treats this issue). For the remaining ten infants the records are about 80% complete. Some of the intervals of missing data reflect technical difficulties that were essentially unrelated to an infant's behavior (see the Appendix). Other gaps in the records were due to an infant's eye occasionally being off camera as he or she briefly turned away from the stimulus field. For the issues under analysis neither source of missing data should have biased the reported findings.

3

Results

In the following sections, the data on the various scanning parameters are presented in the order which best allows for their cumulative interpretation. At times, however, the full implications of some particular scanning characteristic will require reference to several different scanning parameters—and in such cases provisional inferences which are introduced in one section must be left unsupported until the issue recurs during the analysis of another parameter in a later section. This proved to be unavoidable, given an exploratory study of a number of parameters each of which carries implications for a variety of issues.

THE DETECTION OF STIMULUS CHANGE

It seems well established in the literature that from roughly 2 months of age onward infants are capable of detecting visual discrepancies: whether a habituation procedure has been followed, or a target preference technique is used, an altered stimulus usually seems to attract more visual attention (e.g., Cohen & Gelber, 1975; Fantz, Fagan, & Miranda, 1975). However, in most such studies the stimulus change introduced contour alterations throughout many areas of the stimulus, so an infant could detect a "difference" regardless of where he might look. Suppose, however, that the change occurred in only one part of the stimulus array; would it necessarily be detected? If detection requires a direct fixation of the altered area, then it might in fact be overlooked—unless, of course, infants typically scan over all facets of a stimulus on each presentation. On the other hand, perhaps a change in form can readily be detected by peripheral vision; if so, one might expect to find an immediate saccade to an area of change, regardless of where it is located within the stimulus field. The first part of this section examines evidence bearing on these several possibilities. Subsequently, the analysis focuses on the nature of fixations that are directed toward areas of change. Granting the common finding that infants are inclined to look longer at a changed stimulus, is this due to their making *more* fixations, or might it reflect a tendency to hold these "change-attending" fixations for longer intervals?

The Detection Process

As was illustrated in Figure 1, on three occasions during the series of experimental episodes one of the square figures within the stimulus was replaced by an elliptical form. On each of these trials, as well as in the following episode when the figure returned to the square shape, there was a change within the stimulus array. Consider first whether or not these changes generally were detected by the infant subjects.

Figure 2(a) shows the percentage of time spent in looking at the location of the "sometimes changed" figure during episodes in which a change had, and had not, occurred, averaged across nine subjects.[2] On the average, the infants clearly attended more to this particular feature when its shape had changed from that shown in the preceding episode (the difference between the "change" and "no change" episodes is significant at $p < .01$, U test). Figure 2(b) presents a comparable analysis, but now giving the average number of fixations devoted to the sometimes-changing feature. By this measure also, there is evidence that infants were detecting the periodic change in form at a greater than chance level ($p < .01$, U test). Notice that in each analysis the effect occurred both for changes to an

[2]One subject shown the Form A stimulus is omitted from these analyses because the stimulus failed to change, due to technical difficulties (Also, the data base occasionally is attenuated due to intervals of missing data).

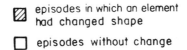

episodes in which an element had changed shape

episodes without change

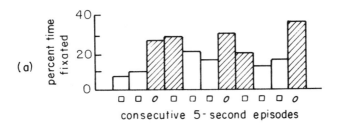

(a)

percent time fixated

consecutive 5-second episodes

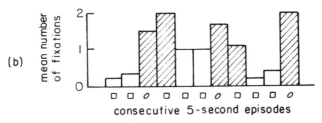

(b)

mean number of fixations

consecutive 5-second episodes

Figure 2.   (a) Percentage of overall viewing time that was devoted to looking at the "sometimes changed" element within the array, averaged across infants. (b) Average number of fixations directed to the "sometimes changed" element.

elliptical form and for changes *back* to a square in the following episode. This argues against a simple "preference for ellipse" interpretation.

The preceding analyses have combined the data from Form A and Form B stimulus formats. Recall, however, that in Form B the change occurred at a location which was close to the infants' locus of fixation at the moment of stimulus presentation, whereas in Form A it was in a peripheral location (see Figure 1). Figure 3 indicates the likelihood that infants had detected the stimulus change under the two different conditions. The same two measures again are used, but now the data from the separate episodes have been combined to allow a direct comparison of reactions to the "change" and the "no change" episodes. By either of the two measures, it is evi-

detected, but failed to attract saccades simply because of its peripheral location—seems less plausible. The issue will be examined further in the Discussion.)

The data in Table 1 indicate just how soon within an episode the change was detected. The findings of interest derive from the Form B stimulus; here it can be seen that the detection of change usually was immediate, in that typically an infant's first saccade within the episode was made directly to the changed feature. Reference to Figure 1 will show that the detected change was located about 5 degrees from the infant's initial direction of regard; evidently some aspect of form perception can readily be accomplished at this eccentricity. In contrast, the changed feature within the Form A stimulus was located roughly 15 degrees peripherally, and at this eccentricity the change in form seemingly went unnoticed.

TABLE 1

Percentage of Episodes in Which the Infant's First Fixation Was Directed to the Location of the "Sometimes Changed" Stimulus Feature. Values in Parentheses Show Numbers of Codable Episodes. Significance Was Determined By the Binomial Test.

Stimulus:	Stimulus unchanged	Stimulus changed	Significance
Form A	1% (21)	3% (15)	N.S.
Form B	11% (9)	63% (16)	$p = .05$

A final point concerns the nature of the change being detected. The "ellipse" episodes were *not* characterized by a pattern of looking back and forth between the square and elliptical forms; rather, a series of several successive fixations were directed to the now-different figure. By implication, infants were responding to a change from the preceding episode, rather than making some sort of "same-different" comparison between two concurrently presented shapes. Furthermore, recall that in the following episode, in which the ellipse was replaced by the more frequently presented square figure, infants again attended more to this location. Since in this case the only quality making this figure "different" was that another shape was in this position during the preceding exposure, it would seem that the infants must have been encoding the *relative locations*, as well as the shapes of the elements. The inference will find further support in a later analysis.

Response to a Detected Change

Numerous studies, using other research procedures, have shown that infants typically respond to a change of stimulus by looking for a longer interval at the altered figure. From a comparison of the patterns shown in Figures 2(a) and (b), it is evident that at least some of this extended viewing time must be due to an increase in the sheer number of fixations devoted to the altered form. Might the increase in viewing time, however, also be due in part to the infants' holding their "change-attending" fixations for relatively longer intervals? Apparently this is not the case. It will be shown in the following section that .7 seconds is a reasonable cutting point for defining an atypically long fixation. Applying this criterion to the data from the four infants who were shown the Form B stimulus, it was found that 29% of their "change-attending" fixations were atypically long; in contrast, the same babies showed a base rate of 35% of such longer fixations when viewing the various elements during episodes of no stimulus change. Not only is the difference not significant, but the direction is opposite to what would be expected if an inspection of the changed element had indeed promoted extended dwell-times. In fact, the detection of change (at least at these ages, and for these stimuli) usually was followed by a series of relatively brief fixations in what appeared to be a rapid survey of the new form.

Many of the preceding effects are illustrated in Figure 4. Represented is the scanning pattern from the first "changed stimulus" episode in the record of the 2 1/2-month-old infant; this was the youngest subject who viewed the Form B stimulus. Notice the direct saccade to the changed figure, and the sequence of several fixations before moving to the unchanged component. This was a typical reaction to the detection of change within the stimulus. Also typical is the occurrence, at seemingly random intervals, of the two relatively long dwell-times in the series of fixations. (Less typical is the fact that most of the calculated fixations happened here to fall very close to figure contours; calibration procedures, or perhaps infant imprecision—see Appendix, section vi—often placed fixations less exactly on figure contours.)

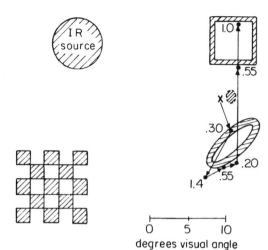

Figure 4. Scan-path of the 2 ½-month-old infant during the first episode in which there was a change within the stimulus. The locus of fixation at moment of presentation is represented by x. Dwell-times are given in seconds.

Summary

Congruent with results based on other observational techniques, it was found that infants will indeed look longer at a changed stimulus—but only if the change is detected, and on present evidence this is likely to occur only if the change happens to fall in an area of the stimulus that regularly is scanned by the infant subject. From present data, it seems that a change in shape can be detected if it is located some 5 degrees in parafoveal vision, but not if it is at an eccentricity of 15 degrees. Maurer and Lewis (1979a) have reported similar effects at 10 degrees, but not at 20 degrees. The typically longer viewing times devoted to a changed stimulus seem due to an increase in the number of separate fixations; apparently the fixations themselves are not held for unusually long intervals.

THE DURATION OF FIXATIONS

For infants to have detected a change within the stimulus, they must have maintained their separate fixations for at least the minimum interval required for an assimilation of the retinal image. The present section will examine the distributions of infants' dwell-times in order to estimate this minimum interval, and to see if it might vary as a function of the nature of the stimulus or the age of the infant. In addition, during each fixation infants must have been setting the parameters that specified the direction and distance of the forthcoming saccade; this must be the case because the two alternative possibilities can be dismissed. It will be shown that saccades were not simply directed at random; and the other alternative, that an entire sequence of directed saccades would be completely specified in advance, seems most unlikely. Estimates will be made of the time required for setting such saccade-directing parameters. Finally, the interrelations between the two inferred processes—the assimilation of current retinal content, and the programming of the forthcoming saccade—will be examined.

The minimum change in the direction of visual regard that could reliably be detected across all scanning records was 1 to 2 degrees of visual angle (see Appendix, section iii). The analysis of infant dwell-times necessarily has been constrained by this measurement parameter, since the data can indicate only the durations of fixations that remained unchanging within these limits. Fortunately, the infant macula subtends about 2 degrees of visual angle, so it can be argued that this is, in fact, a reasonable criterion for defining what constitutes a period of continuous fixation on some particular part of the visual field.

Dwell-Time Distributions

Following the above definition of a continuous fixation, the distributions of dwell-times were determined for fixations directed to elements of the experimental stimuli, and to facets of mother's face. The outcomes are shown in Figures 5(a) and (b). The interval widths for the figures have been expanded just sufficiently to minimize random frequency fluctuations in the distribution profiles. Despite the differing visual contents, the two distributions appear to be highly similar in shape, and are identical in modal value—findings which give added confidence in the generality of observed distribution parameters. (As a rough comparison, the average